THE CAT & FIDDLE
CYCLE CHALLENGE

Edited by Peter Hooper

First published 2018

Cox Bank Publishing Limited
Coxbank, Audlem, Cheshire, CW3 0EU

email: info@coxbankpublishing.com

web: www.coxbankpublishing.com

Copyright © Peter Hooper 2018

ISBN 978-0-9956672-5-9

Printed and bound by Panda Press, Stone, Staffordshire

Turning out of Macc and onto the start of the 'Cat'

Contents

Jason Rourke	Foreword	6
Peter Hooper	Introduction	7
1. Neil Jones	Words	9
2. Jackie Kilding	Cat & Fiddle Challenge	10
3. Martine Grainger	My Cat & Fiddle Day	15
4. Adrian Ryalls	Repton RC's Cat & Fiddle	18
5. Erin Boddice	A Family Day Out	22
6. Ian McDonald	The Glasses	26
7. Jo Holmes	Hijacked!	28
8. Ann Beech	Our Cat & Fiddle story	30
9. Anjam Haling	Our day	33
10. Tony Meredith	Sean Kelly - or not?	35
11. Kevin Palmer	My Cat & Fiddle Story	39
12. Phil Crow	The Cat & Fiddle	44
13. Fiona Jolly	Cramp!	46
14. Chris Nutt	Codsall Photographic	48
15. Paul Richardson	The Bike	50
16. Rob McAuliffe	Cat & Fiddle weekender	54
17. Jenny Prescott	Rourkie's	66
Acknowledgements and photo credits		69

Foreword

The now-famous (or infamous) Cat & Fiddle Challenge was started by my father Brian Rourke in 2002. One of our close friends had a son who had been diagnosed with cystic fibrosis. Possibly out of helplessness, we got our heads together to see if there was something we could do to help. We decided to have a sponsored bike ride to raise money for a Cystic Fibrosis charity with the hope of raising a few hundred pounds, but with the support we received over the years, Rourkie's Challenge has raised well in excess of £650,000 to date. We now work closely with Cystic Fibrosis Care in putting on the event.

It's always a pleasure to be involved in such a well-supported challenge, which owes its success in large part to the hundreds of cyclists who turn out every year – come wind, rain or shine – to complete the 55-mile circuit. What makes the event for many is the chance to ride with world-famous cyclists like Sean Kelly, Jason Kenny and Guy Martin.

I'm delighted that there is now a book which captures some of the inspiring stories from the route – written by first-timers, hardened club riders and those involved on the day. If you contributed a story to the book, then thank you from all of us at Rourke Cycles. And if you didn't, but have a story to share, then send it to Cox Bank Publishing for a future volume.

From my dad and I, thanks to all of you who have made the event so special, so many volunteers, helpers, riders and sponsors. There are too many to name in person, but I will give a special mention to Martine Grainger - we couldn't have done it without her dedication and hard work.

See you all on 'The Cat' soon.

Jason Rourke

Introduction

I can't remember when I first did the Cat & Fiddle Challenge, probably 2008 I think, the year after I'd relocated with my family to south Cheshire from Southampton. I'd rediscovered the joys of cycling in the lanes of Cheshire, the Welsh borders and the Staffordshire Moorlands, and a couple of mates had suggested the C&F as a good outing. And it instantly became one of my favourite rides – an experience shared with most if not all of the contributors to this anthology.

In the past decade I've tried to do the Challenge most years – I couldn't tell you how many times, but I'd guess six or seven. Some years the ride has been easier – like the year I did LEJOG – other years it has been just plain brutal. Sunshine helps. Wind helps or hinders depending on where it is and which direction it's blowing in. Horizontal sleet, hail, rain, thick and chilling fog don't help. Heatwave? If it ever happens I'll let you know...

In 2015 I set up Cox Bank Publishing, with the aim of collecting and publishing writing about sport, physical activity, exercise and outdoor adventure. The C&F Challenge certainly ticks all those boxes. I also wanted to do books (anthologies) about individual events, collecting as many perspectives as possible of a race or an event. My first attempt at this was for the 2016 Potters 'Arf half marathon in Stoke-on-Trent; and I then took the same approach to the 2016 Cat & Fiddle event. In both cases it took a while to get enough contributions to do full justice to the event but having collected stories now over two years – and having been sent some really good writing – it's a real pleasure to be able to bring to you this short anthology documenting what the Challenge means to riders of all ages and abilities. It's a wonderfully diverse set of contributions, capturing all sorts of motivation and drivers for completing the route – from a London cycling club's 'grand weekend away' (and boy, do they know how to party) to a novice sportive rider tackling her first major ride. I hope you enjoy it.

Peter Hooper

Refuelling at Flash Stores cafe

1. Words

Neil Jones

R ain

O oof

U p

R oad

K iller

I nspiring

E xciting

S pecial

M emories!

2. Cat & Fiddle Challenge 2016

Jackie Kilding

I have lived in Cheshire for nearly 30 years and although I have ridden up to the Cat & Fiddle pub from Congleton, Buxton, the Goyt Valley and Macclesfield Forest, for some reason, I had never been up the iconic Cat & Fiddle 'Top 100 Climb' from Macclesfield on a bike. I went up to the closed pub to watch the Tour of Britain in September and saw the amateur cyclists forging a path for their heroes and was a little envious. When a friend told me that he was giving me two weeks' notice to join him on the Rourkie's Cat & Fiddle Cycle Challenge I jumped at the chance. We had never ridden together but had studied each other's form on Strava and concluded that we would be a good match. We had a hilly ride out the week before to test the water and, sure enough, we were very compatible on two wheels. The weather that day was beautiful and a coffee stop was enjoyed with us sitting outside, basking in the autumn sunshine.

I paid my entry fee and saw that the monies were going to the charity Cystic Fibrosis Care. I had worked in the paediatric cystic fibrosis clinic at the local hospital for several years before being pulled out to take on other roles within paediatrics. I had enjoyed my time with the team as well as the children, young people and their families and had some idea of what cystic fibrosis was about. I had some understanding of the impact it has on the whole of the lives of those with it as well as on the rest of the family. I decided that this would be a good opportunity to raise even more money for the organising charity and sent out an email at work and put messages on Facebook. I was perhaps a little unambitious with my target of £100 as I had very quickly reached that mark and will have raised nearly £500 by the time I have collected it all in.

So how did the day go? I had looked at the weather forecast the night before and was dismayed to see that heavy rain was on the cards. The Saturday had been lovely and I hoped that the meteorologists had made an error. Even on waking on the Sunday and finding the ground dry I kidded myself that I was not going to get wet. However, I was not so complacent as to not pack a decent waterproof cycling jacket and Neoprene overshoes.

The parking was good and, as seems to be the way with cyclists, there was some friendly banter with the chaps in the adjacent cars. This mainly consisted of bemoaning the weather as the promised downpour had begun and the roads were already somewhat wet from the deluge. My friend and I had been discussing preparing the night before and how we hoped that we had not left anything essential at home such as shoes. This proved a timely conversation as a voice boomed out asking if anyone had any spare cycling shorts. As the owner of the voice was a male who was probably twice my weight it would be unlikely that any spare shorts of mine, were I to have any, would have fitted anyway. Luckily Rourke's could help him out and I did see him at the finish, no longer sporting jeans and suitably kitted out.

The ride was great and, despite the awful conditions, I thoroughly enjoyed myself; as did my companion. I tend not to start a ride in the rain but, on this day, I did not have a choice and I was mindful of my generous colleagues and friends who were relying on me to turn up and take on the challenge. Now there is rain *and rain*. This was no gentle drizzle. This was relentless, torrential rain which left huge puddles on the road. My jacket kept my body dry but the water coming up from my back wheel soaked the back of my shorts and my glasses were covered in droplets of water. The unabated cloud-burst defeated my waterproof overshoes though. I was glad that I had taken lights, even though it was daytime, as it was quite gloomy and being seen and being safe was important.

Thankfully, by the time we reached Macclesfield, the precipitation had eased and we started up the Cat & Fiddle climb in much better conditions. Little was I to know that crosswinds and fog would replace the wet. The Cat & Fiddle climb is a long uphill drag rather than a steep climb but not having done it before I was not sure what to expect. I did take some satisfaction out of grinding my way past a few fellow cyclists, but I am sure that those who went past me felt the same. I am not the heaviest human being and have a relatively light bike so was taken a little unawares by the cross winds as the road climbed up out of the trees. I could feel myself being pushed sideways as I tried to open up a bit on the slight down hills. Any hopes of seeing the old pub in the distance were dashed by the fog and I was almost at the summit when it came looming out of the murk. A number of cyclists were taking a well-earned rest at the top and it looked as if some had been sensible and talked their nearest and dearest into driving up to meet them with hot drinks. I continued down the hill because I would be too cold stopping in such an exposed location.

The road from Buxton to Leek was hard on the legs after the 7 miles up from Macclesfield to the pub and this too seemed to be a long drawn out uphill slog. We were over half way as the road flattened out so we decided that a hot coffee would be a good idea and stopped off at a small café which was doing a roaring trade with cyclists and motor-bikers sitting cheek by jowl. As ever there were some friendly exchanges and, as seems to be the thing about Brits, the main topic was the weather. Refuelled, we vacated the warmth to be greeted by sunshine and, as we headed towards Leek, we were treated to fabulous views across to the Roaches and Hen Cloud. This demanded a photo stop.

I have fond memories of Leek having worked there as a trainee GP for a year in 1990. It has changed somewhat over the 25 years, and was bustling, but the hill out of the other side had not changed. As we went past the supermarket it dawned on me what we had ahead. There was no chance that I would be flashed by the speed cameras and I am sure the motorists were glad that there was an 'overtaking' lane.

Whilst the ride takes its name from the famous Cat & Fiddle climb, this is something of a decoy as the short but sharp climbs in the second half of the route are every bit as challenging. The cars and buses complicated matters too. I find it hard to climb more slowly than my natural pace and as the cars got slower because of cyclists ahead I was beginning to think that I was going grind to a halt and fall off. I was muttering to myself, 'get past please'. Smallthorne Bank at over the 50-mile mark was not pleasant but was conquered with the joy of summiting at the notorious roundabouts that seemed to cause confusion for one or two of the cars there. Knowing that all the hills were behind me, my friend and I gave a last push for the finish.

We checked in before grabbing a well-earned drink and food. It is a family joke that wherever I go I bump into someone I know and this event was no different. A couple of men I knew from the local gym were there and we laughed together about the appalling conditions. I had a chat with a young man who had travelled over from Leicester on his own to take part for the second time. He had been near me in Leek and we had exchanged comments about the hill ahead.

I did have a very interesting conversation with one of the founders of the Cystic Fibrosis Care charity and she explained how the charity had come into existence and what the funds were used for. We also knew some of the same people from the Stoke cystic fibrosis team.

Did I enjoy the ride? Yes. Would I do it again? Yes. Would I recommend it to any cycling friends? Yes. Did the bad weather spoil it? I am sure it would have been better in dry and sunny conditions, but then it is October and it would not make such a good story.

Jackie nearing the top of the Cat & Fiddle climb

3. My Cat and Fiddle Day

Martine Grainger

Martine is the Midlands community fundraiser for Cystic Fibrosis Care and a leading light in the organisation of the Cat & Fiddle Challenge. We asked her what it takes to make the Challenge the seamless event it is year after year:

Here are some of the things I did in preparation of the Cat & Fiddle:

- Hired a van and collected 800 bottles of water

- Also collected 900 cakes and also got my mom to bake 72 bread puddings.

- Boiled and peeled 144 eggs and grated 30 kilos of cheese

- Collected 120 x 6 cobs and 60 loaves of bread.

- Organised the volunteers at registration, making sure they were all in branded t-shirts.

- Emailed out to all riders (pre-registered) confirmation of entry then email them again with final details

- Try to cover the 'On the day' registration as well as troubleshoot any last-minute hiccups.

- Organised volunteer to take water and food to feed stations.

- Spoke to people about how the Cat & Fiddle was for them.

- Made sure entry fee money was safe at registration

- Try to focus and not to appear shattered from only an hour's kip the night before (but I really slept well Sunday night!)

- Tried to have a permanent smile on my face Sunday – but I did fail in this task quite frequently!

- Comedy moment for me – trying to pick up/collect a rider that was nothing to do with the Cat & Fiddle. I think I scared the poor man. Still brings a smile to my face.

- Strangest request on Sunday – a returning rider asked for a hug – so I gave him a hug.

Jason and Brian Rourke are amazing people and I will continue to work hard and help stage the Rourkie's Cat and Fiddle for as long as they want me involved. The day itself is always fast-paced for the volunteers at registration in trying to get all things done, but we always enjoy it as the riders are wonderful and they all seem up for a bit of banter. We really appreciate everyone's support.

The happy volunteers (Martine front, 3rd from right). Photo courtesy Cystic Fibrosis Care.

4. Repton RC's Cat & Fiddle

Adrian Ryalls

Now if someone at 8am had said 'stuff this let's go home' I have to admit that I would probably have gone, but as usual the Repton RC boys braved the elements and within 30 minutes we were just about warming the water up that had infiltrated our clothes. By this time however, apart from not seeing club member OJ at all – even in Repton (still in his pit I reckon), we were one man down as Nige had decided to go and use an unsuspecting Stoke hedge bottom to talk to Huey, you know what I mean, he had a bit of a bug but got rid of it in the fastest possible way.

Through the main Staffordshire roads we squelched, briefly catching a glimpse of James as he went for a very respectable time for the course along with Sam, we passed famous monuments of the area such as Congleton bypass, and Macclesfield Town FC until we at last reached the start of the Cat & Fiddle climb. It wasn't that bad really, the main issue was the rain and wind, and then visibility as we ascended into the clouds. It was thick wet fog and you could see no further than about 15 feet in front.

After a brief stop at the Cat & Fiddle Inn for an interview with someone with a camera and microphone and some sticky chemical bar we had been given in Stoke (that really does sound dodgy), it was descent time to Buxton through the howling crosswind fog and rain, poor Phil with not much meat on him was blown all over the place and kept calling me a murderer! and I thought he was enjoying it.

Well we thought it was all over at that point with just the A53 descent to negotiate past the Roaches, Leek and back into Stoke

The view from Rourke's Cycles at the start

The famous Sean Kelly stood with Repton RC riders, "and what a top lad he was, thumbs up to him".

but no! Three chuffin' orrible climbs that no-one expected that were a lot worse than the Cat climb.... but at least by Leek the sun had made its first appearance of the day and we grovelled over and back to Rourkie's for tea and medals, and a fair bit of sarnie and cake too.

All safely back at base we posed with Sean Kelly, who once shattered my dreams of being a fast cyclist - because he was so fast in a Paris-Roubaix I once saw live, and I couldn't believe that it was possible to race at that speed all day, I almost gave up cycling!

Nice to be home, dry and showered and just about ready for more adventures in the history of the famous Repton RC! Cheers boys!

Thanks to all who braved the weather and early start, Steve, Kev, Phil, Sam, Nige, Martin, Allen, a great day out. Looks like nice weather in the group photo at the end, well that was four hours after the start, and that was a completely different story as illustrated in the first photo!

In the murk at the top

5. A Family Day Out

Erin Boddice

My name is Erin; I am a member of Wyre Forest CRC. I predominantly race and ride on the circuit, but I enjoy riding cyclocross through the winter to keep my fitness up during the road off season. I am nationally ranked for both cyclocross and circuit racing. I started racing in 2015 and finished third in my first regional race.

In 2016 I completed my first full season of racing and finished third in the West Midlands Youth League. Following my successful results, I was chosen as first reserve for the West Midlands School Games Team at Loughborough University. I have been put onto the Great Britain Cycling Regional School of Racing. The next step on the Team GB Rider Route is the Olympic Development Academy.

I decided to ride the Cat & Fiddle challenge in 2016, because I wanted to support Cystic Fibrosis Care and enjoy a challenging ride with my family. The Cat & Fiddle Challenge is the longest and hilliest ride I've ever done!

The Challenge

It was 6am on the morning of Sunday the 16th of October and we woke up to a cloudless black sky, littered with glistening, polar-white stars. Reluctantly, but remembering the worthwhile cause of this ride, I dragged myself out of my bed and put on just about every item of winter cycling kit I own!

My mum, my dad and I drove to a neighbouring town to pick up my cycling buddy and bacon sandwich provider, Craig. Sure enough the bacon sandwich was ready to go, wrapped in tinfoil and generously topped with ketchup! We continued our journey towards Stoke, the closer we got the greyer the sky became and the thicker the blanket of cloud grew. Then, the absolute biggest cycling nightmare came true... the heavens opened.

We arrived in Stoke and the rain was beating down on the car windows. We fastened our helmets, zipped up our rain rackets, clipped into our pedals and delivered the first pedal stroke. There was no going back now! We battled the rain with unresponsive breaks, dodging every manhole cover, because they had become a one way ticket to sliding across the tarmac! We had a few difficulties finding the start and ended up climbing a few more hills than necessary!

The route was fantastic and we all rode brilliantly as a team, passing slower riders left right and centre. Clear skies were a welcome sight and when the rain subsided, we all breathed a sigh of relief! It was going brilliantly until we got to 'that hill'. We reached the Cat & Fiddle Climb at 25 miles in. I'm an absolutely rubbish climber, and despite being able to talk and breathe with... ease? my legs just wouldn't put the power through the pedals. Craig and my mum rode ahead, ha ha, thanks guys! Luckily my dad stayed with me, offering words of encouragement and motivation. My legs felt like jelly and every time I thought we had reached the top, there was yet another climb. I managed to force a smile come grimace for the photographer. It was such a relief to reach the Cat & Fiddle pub for a well-deserved drink and flapjack! We started what we believed to be our descent. Little did we realise there was more tough climbing to come.

We finally reached the summit of the climb out of Buxton. My dad tells me the views of the Peak District national park were beautiful, but I was too scared I was going to be blown off my bike by the fierce cross wind if my concentration lapsed for just a moment. We glided down the first 14% descent relieved that gravity was working with, not against us. The second descent was even faster: at a 17% gradient we neared speeds of 40mph.

We were 35 miles into the sportive and I could have quite easily stopped there.

I thought that the last 20 miles would be easier and we would have a flat run into the finish. I was wrong. The remaining distance was to be the hardest 20 miles I have done. The rolling hills were the last thing my dead legs needed. And when I really wanted to get off and walk, thankfully my dad was strong enough to give me a helping push up some of the last, sharpest hills. At 45 miles I had a mini meltdown, I was pushed over the edge by a barking Jack Russell, it might sound stupid but dogs are my biggest fear. When my breathing was already laboured the dog made my breaths very shallow and fast. And okay, yes, I started to cry. "I can't do it" I said, my dad said I could. Well I did.

The finish line was a welcome sight, and I helped myself to not one, but two slices of homemade chocolate cake and a helping of mini sausage rolls. I was so happy that I did the ride, and on reflection, I did enjoy it!

55 miles ridden, 3,835ft climbed and 1,501 calories burnt!

Team Boddice at the finish

6. The Glasses

Ian McDonald

Starting my 6th Rourkie ride, I was used to the friendly riders. This year there was more forced laughter as the weather darkened and wind increased. Ride to the start, check in and add extra layers ready for the storm. Where are my expensive riding glasses? Clearly I have dropped them so no choice but to ride on.

Eyes screwed in the rain, it wasn't "like a river" as we climbed the lower Cat, it WAS a river!. Smile at the photographer and try to look strong (!) and then a brief stop in very limited visibility at the top, the polar bears kept back from the road by the crowds. So onward into the mist and Axe Edge with its continuous head wind, glad to be on the top with brief glances at Staffordshire as the clouds started to break.

Sun appearing (shame about my glasses). Stopped at Ladder Edge drink station, outer layers off for a sunny finish, and there hung on my jersey neck were the missing glasses, enjoying their dry ride! So the final 5 miles were all smiles. Looking forward to next year already.

Ian McDonald   Garshall Green, riding my Rourke 631.

Ian (in red) with Russell Horsley "going well on his first ride"

7. Hijacked!

Jo Holmes

OK, where to start? A couple of friends of mine from work (Steve Crombie & Steve Hill) took part in the 2015 Cat & Fiddle Challenge and told me they had a fantastic time, this year (2016) they asked me to come to Burslem to lend a little support to them and I agreed.

I turned up at around 7.20am and came down to the start point at Brian Rourke's cycle shop, Burslem. I might add, I'm not exactly local, I live approx. 20 miles away. The weather at this time was rather good, dry and fairly warm for the time of year. I went to park up, and this was where I met Pat (Kilpatrick) from the Cystic Fibrosis Care charity. I was soon to find out what a lovely lady she is. I went up to her and asked if I could help out as I could see they were just setting up and thought they may need a hand with some of the banners etc. She asked if I wouldn't mind helping with marshalling the car park, gave me a hi-viz and off I started!

I was lucky enough to meet a lovely group of people, and quickly started directing people to the various registration areas and to the main parking area and facilities. I listened as the riders enthusiastically spoke of their experiences, some had done the challenge in previous years, for some it was their first crack at it. Ages ranged from the very young to people of a more a mature age. People came from near and wide to take part, but all shared a love of cycling.

The weather soon took a turn for the worse, it started raining HEAVILY! Some of the cyclist weren't quite prepared for this, but I never really heard one word of complaint. The ladies of Cystic Fibrosis Care were looking after them, supplying cake by the box load!

After most of the cyclists had registered, Pat came to me and asked if they could 'borrow' me for the rest of the day, I said no problem, she said that a couple of the volunteers had unfortunately had to back out at the last minute and could I go up to the Cat & Fiddle with her to take water, cake, energy gels and bottles of water for the cyclists. At this point the rain was still very heavy and the wind had picked up considerably. We had to get up there, no doubt a lot of them would be struggling as it's a fair climb to the Cat & Fiddle, it also didn't help that the pub was closed so no going in for a quick warm and comfort stop.

We got up there and set up, unfortunately we missed some of the riders, but got up there for the majority. The rain had eased a little by this time, but the wind was atrocious! But again, we heard no words of complaint! Bottles were gratefully filled and gels and cake gratefully consumed. Some of the poor souls were extremely cold and I think would have probably given their right arms for a moment or two in front of a warm fire and a warm drink, but they carried on regardless. Again, most were still in very good humour and shared a joke or two, some wished the physios were up there, most wished for nothing more than a hot drink. But there were still hills to climb and downhills to cope with after being cold and wet, a real challenge even for the most hardened cyclist!

After the last few cyclists had come through (and we'd run out of supplies!) we went back to Rourke's. The ladies had been hard at work, there were sandwiches, sausage rolls and cakes by the hundred and much welcomed brews! A very well organised and professional day. I met a lot of fantastic people, hard-working, fun-loving and so friendly, a thoroughly enjoyable day. Can't wait for the next one!

8. Our Cat & Fiddle Story

Ann Beech

It all started for me in 2002, when a friend asked me if I would like to do a charity bike ride for cystic fibrosis as there was a little boy named Alfie Shenton who we knew from our children's school who suffered from the condition. I was really keen to get involved as it was for such a good cause, but then my friend dropped the bomb shell on me that we would only have one month to train for this 55-mile bike ride, and with neither of us having any biking fitness under our belts (except the occasional spinning class), it felt like we were taking on quite a challenge!

When we arrived at Rourke Cycles to sign in on the ride, we were met by Mr Brian Rourke and Roger Shenton (Alfie's Dad). We were the last ones to set off on the ride, but Brian gave us an encouraging "off you go girls, we will catch you up." They soon did catch us up, luckily just as we started the climb up the Cat and Fiddle. Brian, Judith, Roger and Brian's cousin encouraged us all the way up to the top where we stopped off to refuel with coffee and a piece of cake! We were so chuffed that we had managed to get up the bank. Little did we know what was to come on the way home! But somehow, we managed it, even on our clapped out old mountain bikes, we made it all the way.

Once we got back home, we were both buzzing about our achievement, it felt like the best day ever! Anyway, a massive thank you to Brian, as after that, I developed a strong taste for cycling and still ride the Cat & Fiddle every year! If it wasn't for his time and encouragement, and I don't think I would have ridden a bike again after those 55 miles! I now taken different friends and family on the ride who want to have a go, some of

This was us on our first ride in 2002! That's me at the back.

And this is me (centre) with some other friends in 2016.

them hated it, but some of them got the bug like me and continue to cycle till this day, and like me just love riding and being out on my bike. THANK YOU AGAIN BRIAN AND YOUR TEAM FOR ALL THE SUPPORT OVER THE YEARS!

See you next year!

9. Our Day

Anjam Haling

We at Fight Life have been attending Rourkie's Cat & Fiddle Cycle Challenge for the second year now to help with awareness of Cystic Fibrosis.

Rain or Shine!

We love promoting the event and driving up from London to exhibit, spectate, get together with the volunteers and sponsors.

What makes the event for us is interacting with the cyclists before and after the ride - they are always in good spirits and there is always a great atmosphere! We enjoy the banter, endless jokes and distributing drinks at the finishing line.

Our General Manager also likes to attend this event and loves engaging directly to the cyclists.

Why Cystic Fibrosis Care?

Our brand ambassador Jonny Simpson suffers from Cystic Fibrosis and he is also the spokesperson for Cystic Fibrosis Care founded by Ms. Patricia Kilpatrick in 2015.

We have since collaborated with Jonny and CFC to promote public awareness.

Our link to Jonny makes this a cause very close to our hearts.

Jonny Simpson, spokesperson and Pat Kilpatrick, founder, of Cystic Fibrosis Care (in centre)

10. Sean Kelly – or not?

Tony Meredith

I had set off that morning with high hopes and an eye on the weather that forecast it would not start raining until at least 10.00am. As we left Bryan Rourke's shop in Burslem for the Cat & Fiddle Challenge the ominous first spots of rain had started to pepper the pavements and roads of North Staffordshire. By the time we reached the A34 and the outskirts of Congleton, Cheshire the spots had turned to a biblical downpour and any hopes of avoiding being drenched were dashed.

As rider after rider passed me my up-tempo mood had dissipated and began to be replaced by the dreaded psychological mind games intent on me giving up and heading home.

As yet another set of riders passed me I began to realise that this would be a long day and I would earn every mile and metre of gradient that made up the route that day.

"**Morning!!!!** " said the first rider, through the rain and spray that was seemingly ever present, as yet another set of cyclists overtook me in the wet miserable Sunday morning downpour we were all enveloped in and riding through.

"**Hi**" said the second rider as the rest of the cyclists went past in twos, all in perfect synchronicity, looking as if it was no effort at all. I silently cursed under my breath as they passed.

The rain was bouncing off the road and the wind was blowing all other airborne detritus around seemingly at will as the last rider went past me and the mini peloton began to move effortlessly away. The spray off the back wheels drifting in all directions due to the wind but seemingly mostly toward me.

Just then I had a thought. The second cyclist said "**Hi** "but it sounded like an accent I knew was different but I could not place. Then I started to wonder.

Where was that accent from? How did it go again? I replayed the phrase "**Hi**" over and over again in my head.

Surely it wasn't or was that a southern Irish "**Hi**"? Or not? I thought. Was it or was it not?

As the group moved 5 then 10 then 15 yards away from me I had a flash of recognition.

"Jesus!!! That was **SEAN KELLY**!!!" The "**Hi**" was from Sean Kelly.

He actually spoke, and he spoke to me.

The legendary Irish cyclist.

The man Bradley Wiggins had spoken of in awe and said was a hard man and an idol of Wiggins. He had spoken to me. The winner of the Paris Roubaix twice, Milan San Remo twice and seven times Paris Nice race and the green jersey winner in the Tour de France amongst many, many other races all equally hard and formidable.

He had spoken to me!

It may have only been "**Hi**" but it was to me. Just to me.

I now had another thought. You are on a sportive and Sean Kelly is riding the same roads as you. It is wet and miserable and you are soaking wet through to the skin from head to toe. And Sean Kelly just spoke to you.

Do you want to ride with Sean Kelly and his praetorian guard of cyclists?

The answer was "*Yes- of course I do*!!!"

I had no alternative now, I needed to catch the blur of spray and skinny cyclists ahead of me before it was too late and they were gone.

At that moment my mind was made up. I looked down at the wet road between me and them and decided that this was it. I needed to make the gap and forget about everything else. I needed to catch the group ahead at all costs. I needed to dig in and make my legs work harder, my pedals to turn quicker and my bike to move faster than the group in front to have any chance of catching them up.

I increased my tempo and now had a target to aim for.

It was hard work. Very hard work, almost too much for a novice, overweight, middle-aged, born-again cyclist, like me.

I worked as hard as I could and each pedal stroke was a huge effort to try to catch the riders ahead. I changed through the gears to find one that I could get into a rhythm then sub-consciously picked a song I knew and kept time to the pedal revolutions. My speed increased and I kept the song going in my head. I was getting faster and seemingly moving closer.

These guys were not hanging around though and the weather was not kind to any of us. I kept my tempo up as much as I could and began gaining. It took a while but eventually I made the last cyclist in line and then just hung on.

Hanging on to the last cyclist in line I tried to regain my breath and get my heartrate to a somewhat normal level. Inside I cheered and through the sound of my heart pumping in my ears and my tortured breathing I smiled to myself. I was now riding with Sean Kelly.

Or so I thought.

Doubts began to creep into my logic and the basis of my assumptions were being questioned by myself as I was riding at the back of Sean's gang. I tried to look for Sean at the head of the group.

Was that his leg or not? Was he wearing glasses or not? Is that him at the front or not? Would he wear that kind of gear?

By this time we were going up a small gradient and I was looking at the wheel in front of me moving away from me at a slow but gradual rate. I was losing the wheel!!

Damn, damn, damn. I was losing the wheel and did not have the strength or ability to catch up.

I had played my hand and had lived with these boys for a glorious time but now I was losing them. Each pedal stroke left me losing ground. Two yards became 10 yards then into the distance went the group as I struggled to maintain the pace.

That was that, they moved further and further away into the distance. I had nothing left to give and looked forlornly on as they moved further and further up the road. I still had another nearly 30 miles to go and needed to ration my energy to take me all the way to the end.

But.

It was a big but, but I had ridden "*with*" Sean Kelly on a Sunday morning in October 2016.

11. My Cat & Fiddle Story

Kevin Palmer

Why is the Cat & Fiddle Challenge special? First and foremost is the money and awareness it raises for Cystic Fibrosis and the story behind the event is well known. From its conception in 2002 I had ridden the event every year until 2006. Five years, five events, through rain, wind and sunshine.

On a personal level however, 2007 was somewhat different for me. Late in 2006 after enduring years of lower back pain I was finally diagnosed with *spondylolisthesis* which occurs when a bone from the lower spine (a vertebra) slips out of position over another below it.

It answered questions for me, as to why I could ride for several hours at a time with no pain, yet upon standing upright the pain would immediately return.

My consultant explained that the position on the bike helped relieve the pressure on the nerves whereas standing or walking for prolonged periods of time would inevitably bring back the pain.

Having exhausted all other treatments, surgery would be necessary to correct it; I then faced two options, to continue managing the pain leaving surgery until later in life as the condition worsened.

The second was to have surgery immediately where at the age of 47 the odds were in my favour of a better recovery.

With that in mind along with a good success rate, I made my decision and in May 2007 underwent surgery for decompression & fusion L1 & L2 vertebrae; I won't detail the procedure other than to say that medical grade steel plates and screws now play a part in holding together my lower spine.

After several weeks of physiotherapy and repeated exercises to get me mobile again, I eventually made my attempt to get back on the bike.

To tie this in with the Cat & Fiddle Challenge, prior to surgery I had set myself the goal to ride this event which takes place in October.

A few short rides later however, reality had struck home and it quickly became apparent that the October goal was never going to be achieved.

With my head awash with negative thoughts and self-doubts I decided at that point to take a break from cycling, a break that was to continue for seven years.

Fast forward now to June 2014 when two significant things happened;

Firstly, I was sent a 'Well Man' letter to arrange an appointment at my local Group Practice for my human MOT check, the results showing cholesterol just north of ideal with a weight gain to match it.

Secondly, a copy of Cycling Weekly was dropped onto my desk by my boss, significant in having not read an issue since May 2007, the year I had surgery.

No ordinary issue mind, with a feature on Team Sky training in Yorkshire as the Tour de France was to start in Leeds a month later, I read it from cover to cover and something clicked...

Inspired to get the bike (poly wrapped and covered up for seven years) out on the road again, I decided to try a few short rides.

Having forgotten to stop eating and my old club jersey looking slightly pear shaped, the excess weight I was carrying slowed my progress and things were not easy at first. With a change in diet along with good weather, within a few weeks I had completed several rides with the longest for the year being a 47-mile circuit I first rode when I was 16. I was enjoying the bike again, my weight started to drop and more importantly I was experiencing no pain in my lower back.

Things progressed rapidly in 2015 with the Cat and Fiddle Challenge goal I had set as a target in 2007 finally happening that year, a good event run in cool but dry conditions.

2016 however was a little different as on the morning of the ride with the rain coming down sideways it would have been very easy to stay in bed. Trying my best to ignore the inclement weather, I set off from home to register for the event.

Although wet the flat run to Macclesfield was quite pleasant as at least for this section of the ride you had the wind on your back. Leaving the town on Buxton Road is where the ride really starts as you start to breathe heavier and try to find a rhythm that mirrors how you are feeling on the day.

The first section of the climb meanders through a canopy of trees before the landscape opens up revealing the vista that is the Peak District and it was around this point I met up and had a brief chat with Brian Rourke who appeared to be coaching a young rider, in very good hands I thought to myself.

Further up the climb you get a chance to catch your second wind as it levels out and even descends slightly before the final upward section towards the summit where the public house from which the climb takes its name was today shrouded in mist.

Taking a brief stop at the top I spotted Sean Kelly who after being interviewed set off on the descent towards Buxton. At one point I was close behind as I watched him along with two other riders negotiate the tricky bends and disappear into the misty distance, his experience as an ex pro clearly evident.

Turning right on to the A53 towards Leek was where I managed to latch onto the Kelly group again as you start the climb up to

Axe Edge. It was here that I started chatting to a young rider, George Spooner who had travelled up from London to ride the event; at 16 with 40 years between us it was wonderful to see youth not being wasted.

Continuing towards Leek with the weather now starting to improve I eventually found myself beside the man himself, Sean Kelly. Here was a guy that had won Paris-Nice seven times, five Tour de France green jerseys plus countless one day classics and here I was riding alongside him. Chatting briefly and joking about the weather it was one of the pinnacles of my return to cycling.

We stayed together for this leg of the journey until the climb out of Leek where Sean and a few others stopped at the water station.

Young George and I decided to continue on, negotiating the last few climbs until we finally arrived at the finish. By now we were dried out by the sun that had finally made an appearance and ready for the superb refreshments laid on for us.

Yes, the Cat & Fiddle challenge is special, its connection with Cystic Fibrosis Care, the time of year it is run (which adds to the challenge) and the number of ex-pros both male and female plus the odd celebrity who turn out to ride it making it so.

As for me personally, it will always be connected with my return to cycling after the seven years away from riding the bike. For that alone I give thanks to my Consultant Mr E B Ahmed for the superb job he did on my back, to Karen my wife who was my rock following surgery and finally to Steve Nixon (my boss) for that inspirational copy of Cycling Weekly!

12. The Cat & Fiddle

Phil Crow

Ridden this ride for the last five years - always come back for it as I'm originally from Newcastle (I'm now in Lincoln) so it's good to come and ride my old area.

Also, happy to support Cystic Fibrosis Care as my nephew died of it seven years ago, so it's a good thing to do for my sister who's now in New Zealand. Keeps Fletcher in my mind.

The Cat & Fiddle has for me got progressively more enjoyable which means I must be getting a wee bit fitter each year- it's a lovely area to ride whatever the weather and I'll be back each year to support this event- just need to buy a Rourke bike now....!

13. Cramp!

Fiona Jolley

I'm a member of Kenilworth Wheelers and 2016 was my second year of riding the event, so I was ready for the climbs but not quite prepared for the torrential rain, fog and winds... (I had, however, been sensible enough to put dry clothes in my car for the drive back to Warwick). I entered as a solo rider and was helped along by a lovely local who gave me a pull over the top away from the worst of the winds (little ladies get battered more easily was my excuse - thanks Bob).

After pushing on through the bad weather and only stopping briefly for some slightly soggy home-made flapjack, I made it back and headed straight to my car to change into dry clothes and get warm. Trying to peel off my very wet Lycra was not dissimilar to removing a wet suit, which I was trying to achieve modestly in my car in the car park. Half way through the most delicate and risky part of the operation, I was struck by horrific thigh cramp. This had the effect of throwing me into a spasm of shapes whilst trying at the same time not to attract attention or further display my already not quite covered privates. Thankfully, I think my car disco moves went mostly unnoticed, and I managed to set off on my drive home without too much of a red face. Thanks to all those volunteers who stood out in that horrific weather to support us cyclists and a great charity.

Fiona and friend, 2015 Cat & Fiddle

14. Codsall Photographic

Chris Nutt LRPS

It was back in late September 2010 that we had the call from Martine asking if we would be able to cover the photography at the Cat & Fiddle Challenge. And what a day it was. The rain was horizontal, cold and unrelenting – I suppose a fairly typical late Autumn day in the Staffordshire Moorlands and Derbyshire Peaks! Despite wearing what was supposed to be waterproof clothing I was soaked to the skin within half an hour. On most photo assignments this would have been the end of our coverage, normally to protect our equipment rather than ourselves. However, the cheerful nature of the riders passing by – who by that time had done about 80% of the climb, was infectious. I saw smiling faces and waving hands – and even heard cheery shouts from some of them – even though it must have been some of the worst possible conditions to be taking on such an arduous ride. Due to the cross-wind a couple of unfortunate guys crashed into each other a few hundred yards from where we were taking the photos – I ended up taking their cycles back to Rourkie's – whilst they were shipped to the local hospital. Some of the riders who purchased photos told us they brought them as they wanted a record of the day as they had never cycled in such appalling conditions. Brave guys.....

So, our introduction to photographing Rourkies C&F Challenge was "interesting" – but gave us an appetite to see if we could at some point take photos of the riders in sunshine. Fortunately, the following years did give us better weather (with the exception of the 2016 ride!) and the opportunity to capture some of the stunning scenery in the photos. The ride is always a pleasure to cover – even if it is often cold and damp up on the tops.

However, it also gives us the opportunity to raise some funds for a great charity to which we have some personal "connections". My school friend's sister had cystic fibrosis and unfortunately didn't make it past her teens. That sad event dramatically raised my awareness of CF. In more recent years a friend's daughter also suffers from CF, but thanks to the tremendous leaps forward in treatment over the intervening 20 years is leading a reasonably normal life. Let's all hope that medical advances will one day see a cure for this cruel illness.

After hours of photographing cyclists in fog and rain, this is the view after the last cyclist had vanished up the hill...

15. The Bike

Paul Richardson

Browsing the magazines in Tesco recently I decided, on a whim, to buy Cycling Weekly for the first time in over 20 years. Little did I know what it would lead to.

Once I saw the entry form for this ride I knew I was doomed. Having seen that Guy Martin (my daughter's a big fan) and Sean Kelly (I watched him monster many an Alp, back in the day, on bikes that would hurt modern riders a lot) were doing it, I was in!

I sent in my entry, sitting at the PC with the sun streaming through the window and warming my back nicely. Hmm.

Having taken up cycling again a year ago at 61, 25 years after I last seriously rode, I thought it would be a good challenge. I knew all the route to Leek well, and remembered, badly as it turned out, that it was a relatively flat run back from Leek to Stoke.

In the last two weeks, the nearer the day came the less I slept, as I had been up 'the Cat' for the first time at the start of October.

On the day I woke feeling surprisingly good, set off, picked up my riding companion (let's call her Jackie, as that's her name) and set off to park up at the start. Just as we arrived at the car park (8.15am-ish) it decided it was time to start raining heavily. Kitting up was therefore all done in the pounding rain and off we rode to the start proper arriving already nicely wet.

And so off we set, riding into the driving wind and rain. My first challenge at 10 miles was riding past my home. I must admit I did give it a longing look thinking how warm it would be inside.

Once past Congleton and out into the country the ride proper began. On a drink stop at Fools Nook (just over the canal bridge) I think Sean Kelly Passed in a large group. At some point around this time, a bike passed me and with the quick glimpse I got I thought it was the same as mine. Now this may not seem like much of a big deal, but in the 30 years I've owned a CIÖCC bike (steel and now carbon) I've never seen another on the road. Carrying on to Macclesfield we deviated from the route slightly. At the start of the Silk Road we forked left and then right at the first lights. The benefit of this was it kept you off the busier Silk Road and allowed a pit stop opposite the station prior to starting 'the Cat'.

The early section of the climb wasn't quite as bad as my previous attempt as I was passing quite a few people which always makes you feel better. Jackie was off up the road at this stage. Also, Strava was telling me I was two minutes up on my best time. That didn't last long though.

Once away from civilization the road became more exposed and turned into the wind. It didn't take long for the two minutes gained to be wiped out and pain to become a constant companion. The only good thing was the low cloud stopped you seeing the top and therefore how much of the climb was still to go.

Before the top there is a café. As cold and wet as it was, a highlight there was a young girl standing out in the rain shouting "well done and thank you for riding". Bless. While still smiling at this I passed the driveway leading to the café where there was a guy slumped on his bike. As I approached a plaintive cry of "how far is it to the top" came from him. He was so close, but didn't have any idea where he was, one of the problems of the mist.

On my way down the hill towards Buxton, and a reunion with Jackie, I was thinking constantly about the ride up Axe Edge. I had built this up to such a monumental climb in my mind that in reality it was just a long, cold drag up to the haven of Flash Bar Stores. As I rode up to the Bar Jackie, who once again beat me up the climb (power to weight is a real pain sometimes) pointed towards two riders just leaving and let me know that indeed the bike I thought was like mine was the same (white CIÖCC Rydon). Thrilled by the news I'd once again just missed the chance to compare notes we had a nice warming brew.

The run into Leek was fairly uneventful but with the added bonus of the massive downhill past the Roaches and the knowledge that all the hard climbs were done. Little did we know.

Turning left out of Leek feeling relieved all the hard work was behind us we encountered the first of a series of four very unpleasant bumps in the road.

These four little digs, at Ladder Edge, Endon, Norton Green and Smallthorne were just a nasty little end to a long wet, cold ride. The upside for me though was that on these hills, helped by some bad timing at traffic lights by Jackie, I managed to get to the top first for a change. AND THE SUN WAS OUT.

After this it was just the short run into the finish and grab whatever I could find to eat. My left foot was aching and I was cold but happy.

I had a hunt around for the other CIÖCC rider, but he must have already gone.

Will I be there next year? Damn right I will. Happy days.

16. A Cat & Fiddle weekender

Rob McAuliffe

This 2016 Brixton Cycles trip had, rather unwisely, been billed as an end of season *Ronde van Calderdale* and in short it certainly delivered certain aspects of that Hallowed April Classic.

The Cat & Fiddle Challenge is organised by Brian Rourke in aid of Cystic Fibrosis Care and the large attraction of the ride - apart from the stunning scenery; the chance to escape London for a day; and the large opportunity to drink some lovely, cheap ale - is that Guy Martin and Sean Kelly do the ride, both of them having a close connection with Rourke.

Unfortunately, Guy Martin was 'held up in China' and couldn't attend. It later turned out that he had got wind that BC's very own Emma-Jane was attending and was too scared to turn up. Sadly Emma bottled it too. In a carefully constructed act all week, she convinced us that she was simply too ill to travel, let alone ride. This was gloriously exposed by Strava as a ruse to go riding with her new beau in Kent, rather than us bearded lovelies, in Stoke. Another missing member was Saffron who had to cancel as there were babies' heads to kiss at christenings and even though she had tried every trick in the book to get herself out of it, the guilt wore her down and she was a DNS.

Due to several life commitments the group's travel up to Stoke was split up throughout the day. Joe and Matt had gone up to see family in the area the preceding day, Bruce had been doing something called 'running' in Oxford and was driving, Tim and James (Jimmy) were on the early train and myself and Adam on a later train. The plan was to find a nice little pub and to all meet up about 8pm, have a civilised meal and get a relatively early night. As expected, this is EXACTLY what happened.

Starting as they mean to go on...

The two train crews' plans had played out wonderfully and Jimmy and Tim had arrived at the hotel, checked in and found a pub as Adam and I arrived. Everyone had warmed themselves up with a few train beers and the warm pre-ride, pre-beer glow had descended upon us. Adam and I discovered that the chaps had taken a room already, so we played room lottery with who we would get. Jimmy lost and got me and I immediately set about hiding or dismantling parts of his bike and kit.

After I had finished breaking his chain down into individual links, Adam and I met up in reception and with the help of a lovely receptionist from Bolton, we booked a taxi to the Newhop Inn, safely arriving at 8pm to find the newly arrived Joe, Bruce and Matt tucking into some very reasonably priced pints of Bass with the already well lubricated Tim and Jimmy.

After a few rounds of the irresistibly cheap beer, we used the power of Jimmy's internet to find a well-reviewed local curry house and set off on foot to locate it. With the curry house duly found at the first attempt and a table for seven sorted out, we set about the menu with gay abandon, fuelled by the wonderfully named 'Mongoose' lager. The staff were very considerate and just kept bringing us beer, even though we hadn't ordered it. From what is remembered of the food, it was very good and large quantities of it had been consumed, a perfect athlete's dinner. With the food duly dispatched it was a taxi job back to the hotel to check if the wedding reception, that Adam had spotted earlier in the hotel, was still going strong.

It was decided that as the wedding reception had moved through into the hotel bar, we should join them for a nightcap. The wedding party was made up of several Battersea Wanderers players, which was an odd blast from the past for yours truly. As we were all aware that the ride the next day was an unknown quantity, it was decided that we should just drink whisky until 3am......thanks Joe.

The next/same morning we were all greeted with proportional headaches and playful stomachs. As people filtered down to breakfast the damage was clear. Luckily the weather was appalling, so we had bigger things to worry about. Joe, who had led the whisky charge the previous evening, had a unique remedy for his state. That remedy was to eat the entire breakfast buffet and to be offended when this was pointed out to him by the rest of the group as "I thought I'd been pretty conservative to be honest". After Joe had polished of the restocked tray of sausages we assembled in reception to leap outside into the raging maelstrom that Stoke was providing for us. As sign-on was open to 10.30am, we had actually timed it pretty perfectly and rolled out with the storm dying and the wedding fayre at the hotel being assembled around us.

As we rode up the hill, through the industrial estates and past all of the fast food restaurants, there was silence in the group, as stock was being taken and mental damage reports were being compiled.

We reached sign-on safely and after some confusion about whether we had already completed the ride or not, as we were the last to sign up, we were off and rolling through the beautiful town of Burslem. There genuinely isn't a lot to say about the first 20 miles of the route as it just involves an A road smash to Gawsworth, then some nicer lanes to Macclesfield. Joe was in his element though as it was true tester country. Myself and Joe were left hunting potatoes off the front by the rest, not as a racing plan, but because neither of us had mudguards...

Eventually we reached Macclesfield, which was emotional for Joe as it is where he had several of his worst tattoos done as a younger man. The climb that gives the ride its name starts immediately from Macc town centre and doesn't stop for the next 7-ish miles. It's not steep *per se*, but it drags and drags and even has some descents in it; the thing that makes it truly challenging is the weather. This road can as easily be closed in summer as winter due to the changing weather or wind. The road twists and turns into and out of the wind and keeping a steady pace is very hard, whether you are in a group or not, as effort is increased into the gale for no reward in forward velocity.

The BC group quickly split as the whippets, led by Tim and Adam left Joe (who actually has the fastest time in BC of 30m-54s up the hill, probably set when he was fleeing a tattoo studio), Bruce and myself behind. I was quickly binned by Joe and Bruce, and Joe continued up the road solo leaving me to mark pace against Bruce. On the lower slopes we all just concentrated on survival and as the climb gains altitude the sections of flat and small descents give some respite. On one of these sections I caught Bruce and thus precipitated a classic Contador vs Schlek climbing battle. Punch and counter punch were thrown as we vied for superiority, all of this taking place at a heady 9mph. Finally in a daring attack I pushed the pace to 11mph and Bruce was left in the wind. The rest of the climb is a fight against the wind and the gradient but eventually we all made it up to the Cat & Fiddle pub, which was sadly closed.

Upon arrival it was clear that the 'big boys' had gone hard. 1,000 yard stares were in abundance. Something had snapped inside Matt, and Tim and Adam were looking a touch puce. Jimmy was irritatingly chipper and Joe was already thinking about lunch. It transpired that Adam and Tim had shelled the rest and had actually had a proper ding-dong up the hill, it was later

established that Tim had put 5s into Adam, to win nothing but everlasting respect.

The top of the Cat is bleak, it was windy, rainy and cold and the brave volunteers giving out gels and drinks that tasted like cold Lemsip were greatly appreciated.

So we'd pretty much done it then yeah? Just ride back down and go back to Stoke, simples.......

As we left the Cat & Fiddle we were all looking forward to what promised to be a magical descent. It turned out to be more climbing.

The murk at the top

The fast lad's effort and the slow lad's lack of effort on the main climb had added some balance to the pace and we all chugged up the moor line astern. We had been passing fellow riders for a while on the main climb as we slowly picked up the main groups of the sportive. People were not in good places, there was a magnificent variety of bikes and kit on display and the brave souls who were on MTBs with running shoes were finding it tough going. Finally we crested the moor and the descent to Buxton. This isn't even a tenth of the climb as we would be turning right and heading over the shoulder of the moor to Leek. Needless to say we enjoyed what there was and Jimmy took great delight in ignoring the massive KEEP LEFT sign and using all of the available road.

At the bottom we took the right and continued uphill, into a headwind on a well trafficked road. The group broke up again and it became clear that Matt and Bruce were suffering, mainly from their hangovers. This left me in the unenviable position of trying to hold on to Tim, Jimmy and Adam. Adam and Jimmy toddled off and left me and Tim to it. As we ground our way up the hill we came across one poor chap who had clearly spent a lot of money on a new aero bike and 90mm wheels, which he was having a whale of a time controlling in the gusts of wind. His fighting of the bike became so animated as we reached him that Tim was involuntarily caused to shout "EASY, WHERE ARE YOU GOING?" as the poor lamb nearly wobbled into the verge and down an 8 ft. drop.

We regrouped at the Round Table pub and the damage done to Matt and Bruce became clear to the rest of the group. So we did the only decent thing and had a proper smash up over the next bit of moor and finally the long descent. The wind was nagging us though and even though the rolling descent was fast, it was still a considerable effort. That was until we came across our third DANGEROUS DESCENT sign. Now, we had accidentally

At last - the sun appears en route to Leek

ignored the first two. So we threw ourselves into this one at a rate of knots. It wasn't that dangerous but it was bloody steep and most of the group touched nearly 50mph on the way down.

The road rolled into Leek and I took myself off into a pub straight out of the League of Gentleman to do what normally gets done in fields. When I had emerged Matt and Bruce had arrived and we once again set off. We had 10 miles left, but we were warned that there were some hills.... the road rolled and rolled and there were more hills that we dragged ourselves up. Eventually we regrouped in a bus with about four miles to go. Matt was AWOL and we waited. He appeared looking very grey and announced "sorry, it's just that for the last 15 miles I've been being sick in my mouth and swallowing it".

Two hills later, a dropped chain and some traffic chaos, we arrived back at Brian Rourke's shop and rolled into the community centre's car park. Sean Kelly was there watching us roll in and in such company Jimmy decided to get all his tricks out and duly pulled some sick air (maybe 2 cm) off a speed bump while shouting "YIPPEE!" Kelly nearly choked on the ham butty he was scoffing. We signed back in and attacked the buffet with vigour. Bruce nearly lost his food to a cheeky cat and Matt had to have a little collapse on a table.

We were then interviewed on camera, by the lovely lady whose daughter lived in Brixton, the main reason for the interview appeared to be that 'we had come all the way from Brixton'. People from Stoke are very impressed by a 1.30 hr train journey it seems. We had a look around the shop and 'Kelly's Bar' upstairs and then headed back to the hotel. We were kindly given free run of the showers in the health club and some of us started to feel a bit more human. Matt was not one. Post showers we met in the bar and formulated an eating plan over some nursed beers. It transpired that there was a Toby Carvery down the road (Joe magically knew this.....) so off we trooped to 'Stoke Marina'. Bruce took his leave to drive home to MK at this point and after fighting our way past Quasar, Ten Pin, Cashino and Costa we came across Stoke's version of Monaco Harbour, it was quite something.

En route Jimmy let slip that his first job was as a children's party organiser at Ten Pin. A Toby Carvery was a new experience for some of the group, but no one held back, including the brave Matt who took the 'kill or cure' option with the food. Nearly all went supersize and some serious dents were made in the buffet cart.

Several pints later we retrieved our bikes and rolled down to the station, after an argument about which route was quicker. This lead to one group taking the dual carriageway, and another the canal. Both groups arrived slap bang at the same time.

Beers were then required for the journey and with Tim convinced he could find a Waitrose or Fortnum & Mason concession in suburban Stoke, it was left to myself and Adam to clean a local offy out of Guinness, San Miguel, Monster Munch and beef hula hoops. Unfortunately, the train was rather busy but after some faff we got all the bikes and people together in one place. Joe promptly fell asleep and Adam got very angry about how the train took 3hrs to get to London. Thankfully before he had an aneurism, he was distracted by his beef hula hoops and how the smell of them stayed on his fingers.

Matt, emboldened by his attack on the carvery bowed to pressure and had a Big Mig, which transformed him and brought him back from the brink. Eventually the train arrived in Euston and the group headed out on to the London Streets. The main group quickly broke away and weren't seen again after Waterloo Bridge, thus with their tail lights blinking into the darkness, another very enjoyable BC trip was brought to a close.

Same again next year, but with less whisky.

17. Rourkie's

Jenny Prescott

Memories of the 2016 day from those of us waiting at home for the safe return of our plucky riders!

So today's the day? All those weeks of texting us (me and Bertie Border) that you were doing the ride and we had to keep the day free — that's for today?

All that prep last night, making sure 'the' bike was in tip top condition, that you had everything (and more) that you could ever need for the journey there and the ride itself... that's for today?

That's why the alarm went off at 5.30 am then? Out of bed before I could (dutifully if reluctantly at such an hour!) offer breakfast ...showered, shaved and out of the door within the hour.

Three hours later, texts to confirm safe arrival, weather reports, numbers of competitors - Bert and I could only walk the fields and wonder how things were going as the rain poured down here.

Friends arrive for tea as your texts arrive to say you are just leaving, the day successful if a little soggy!

Bert waiting by the door for you in the cosy warmth of the house, dinner simmering 'til you get home...then radio traffic reports of tailbacks and delays.

And now here you are complete with sodden clothes, your mud splattered bike, all the bits and bobs packed last night scattered all over the floor to be put away by one of us!

'What a day,' you say, 'Fantastic crowd, exciting route!' you're soaked but happy— and then, 'Must keep the date free for next year's Cat and Fiddle Challenge...'

Acknowledgements and photo credits

First and foremost, thanks are due to all the contributors to this book for allowing the use of their writing. Special thanks to Brain Rourke Cycles (especially Jason Rourke) and to Cystic Fibrosis Care for their support and encouragement. Three faces which all riders of the Cat & Fiddle Challenge will know are CFC's Pat Kilpatrick and Martine Grainger and Codsall Photographic's Chris Nutt, all of whom have been especially helpful in the genesis and production of this book. Thanks too to Gaz Williams of Foley Creative for original artwork and to John Mainwaring of MarketingBiDesign for the cover design. And finally our thanks to Erin Boddice of Bewdley School in Worcestershire, for helping in the production of this book as part of some voluntary work experience she did with us. And for contributing her very own Cat & Fiddle story too!

Photo Credits – images courtesy of:

Pages 3, 8, 60 – Peter Hooper
14, 27, 31 (bottom) 42, 49, 59, 66 – Codsall Photographic
17 – Cystic Fibrosis Care
19,21 – Adrian Ryalls
25 – Erin Boddice
31 (top) – Ann Beech
34 – Fight Life/Cystic Fibrosis Care
41 – Kevin Palmer
45 – Phil Crow
47 – Fiona Jolley
53 – Paul Richardson
55, 58, 62, 63, 64, 65 – Rob McAuliffe
67 – Jenny Prescott

Also from Cox Bank Publishing:

'Arf Marathon

The story of a half marathon, the ever-popular Potters 'Arf, with contributions from over 60 participants: runners, walkers, volunteers, organisers, charities and more. In support of the Dougie Mac and Donna Louise charities.

Just a Face in the Crowds

By life-long Stoke City supporter Roger Horwood: his memories, spanning seven decades, of watching football's greatest like Stanley Matthews and George Best. In support of the Sir Stanley Matthews Coaching Foundation.

SPLASH!

An anthology of swimming poetry and artwork from Hillside Primary School, SPLASH! is designed to be a writing and drawing book too. Make the book your own. In support of the Royal Life Saving Society.

Sporting Stories

Over 80 contributors tell their stories of what physical exercise means to them. With more than 30 sports and activities covered, there's inspiration for all – and some great artwork too. In support of three great good causes.

Order online at www.coxbankpublishing.com/shop